The Girl & Her Magic Bows

_ By Donatella DeLaRosa

MISNER AND MONROE PUBLISHING

The Girl & Her Magic Bows

Illustrations by Jade Jupiter

Misner and Monroe Publishing, First Edition
2024

Printed in the United States of America

Hardcover:
ISBN-13: ISBN: 978-0-9992632-3-5

Softbound:
ISBN-13: 978-0-9992632-6-6

eBook:
ISBN-13: 978-0-9992632-5-9

Library of Congress Control Number:
TX9-424-079

Acknowledgement:

To my parents, who have always inspired me to believe that the sky is not the limit, but just the beginning.

To my grandparents, for my sense of humor and reminding me "How Loved I am."

To my older brothers, for torturing me in the name of "toughening me up."

To Mrs. Buerstatte, for her never-ending kindness and support.

To Mrs. Krause, for always believing in me and encouraging my potential.

To Dr. Dillon, for keeping me in line and pushing me to be my best.

To Mr. Hayes, for his intellectual insight and wisdom.

To Mrs. Gomez, for her passion for creativity, the arts, and teaching me how to articulate them together.

And to all the young women who bravely embrace every challenge with courage, determination, and unwavering spirit.

Once upon a time, there lived a young girl named Dona. She lived in a small town in Idaho.

Her Mom, Dad, and brothers all loved her very much, in part because she was so sweet and kind.

But what was truly remarkable about Dona was her very special set of bows with magical properties. The bows, which had been used by her mother, were given to her by her grandmother.

Dona's grandma said that she would put on her magical bows whenever her mom got nervous about anything.

Dona came to realize
that these very special bows
would give her the strength to
overcome any new challenge she
faced. Each time she placed one
of these bows on her head, she
could embrace the challenges,
new experiences and overcome
her fears.

Let's join Dona on her daily
journey as she dons her bows
while achieving childhood
milestones and entering
adulthood.

On Dona's first day of potty training,

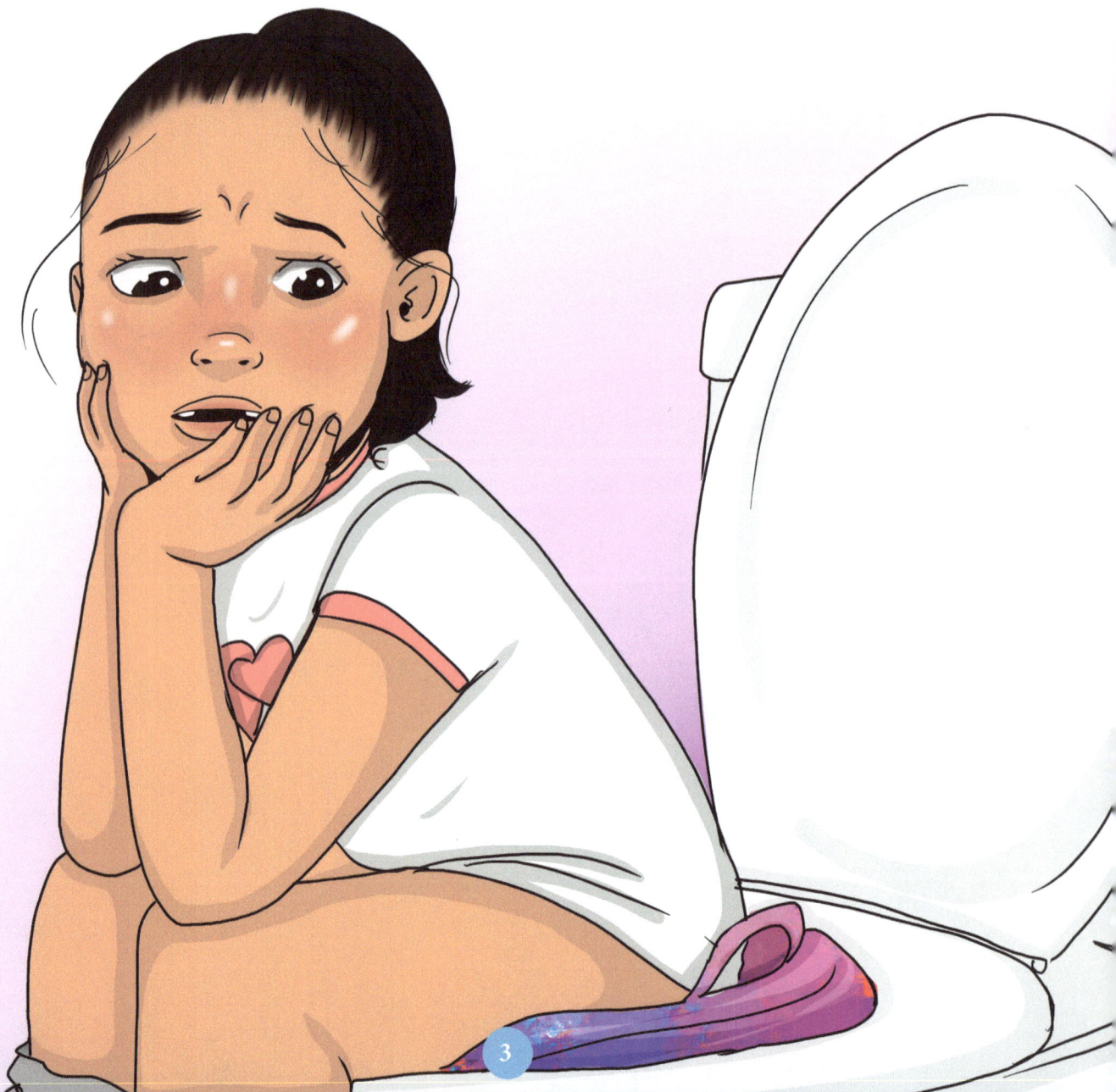

Her mother brought out a vibrant purple **POLKA DOT** bow and gently placed it in her hair.

Admiring herself in the mirror, Dona felt she **could do** anything!

From that moment on, she celebrated each successful trip to the bathroom while wearing that beautiful bow.

Dona got a new bike on her birthday but didn't know how to ride it.

Scared, she reached into her collection for a bright GREEN BOW and wore it for confidence.

After a short time, that confidence helped her ride her bike on her own. Soon, Dona was riding like a real pro!

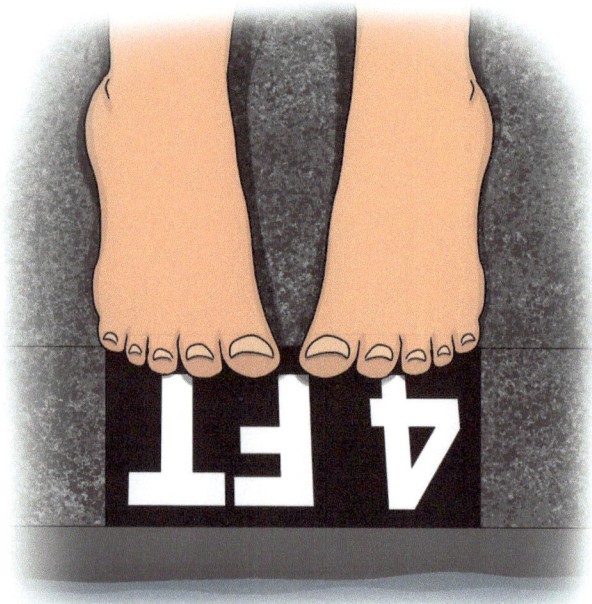

When Dona went to the local pool with her family, she took out a beautiful **BLUE BOW** from her backpack and put it on her head. After a deep breath at the pool, she plunged into the cool water.

Dona splashed and played with the other children in the pool as her mother looked happily on.

For her first day at school, Dona wore her PURPLE BOW.

"I love your purple bow!" a classmate who approached her during recess said. "Do you want to play?"

Dona was happy that she had made a friend on her very first day at school.

One day, Dona's family introduced her to a strange new food called spaghetti. Wearing a radiant **RED BOW,** the food looked delicious to Dona. Though she had been concerned about splattering the tomato sauce on her white shirt, she expertly rolled the strands of spaghetti onto her fork and managed to eat them without getting any sauce on her shirt.

For Dona's first time on an airplane, she wore a lovely **PINK BOW.**

Gazing out the window with a sense of awe and wonder, she thoroughly enjoyed every moment of her first airplane ride. It was as if all the anxiety she had previously imagined just melted away.

When Dona's grandmother was on her way to visit with a new puppy, Dona was at first afraid to hold the cute puppy.

Seeing her YELLOW BOW glowing from its place in her dresser drawer, Dona quickly attached it to her hair.

After her grandmother arrived with the fluffy puppy, Dona hugged and played with the little dog as if they were old friends.

For her first sleepover at the home of her friend Natalia, Dona wore a vivid **ORANGE BOW** from her collection

To her surprise, her shyness seemed to have disappeared. Feeling warm and fuzzy, she played with Natalia, her baby brother, and her toys for hours.

For Dona's first visit to a dentist to have her teeth cleaned, she wore the soothing **TURQUOISE BOW** from her collection. Holding her mother's hand tightly at first.

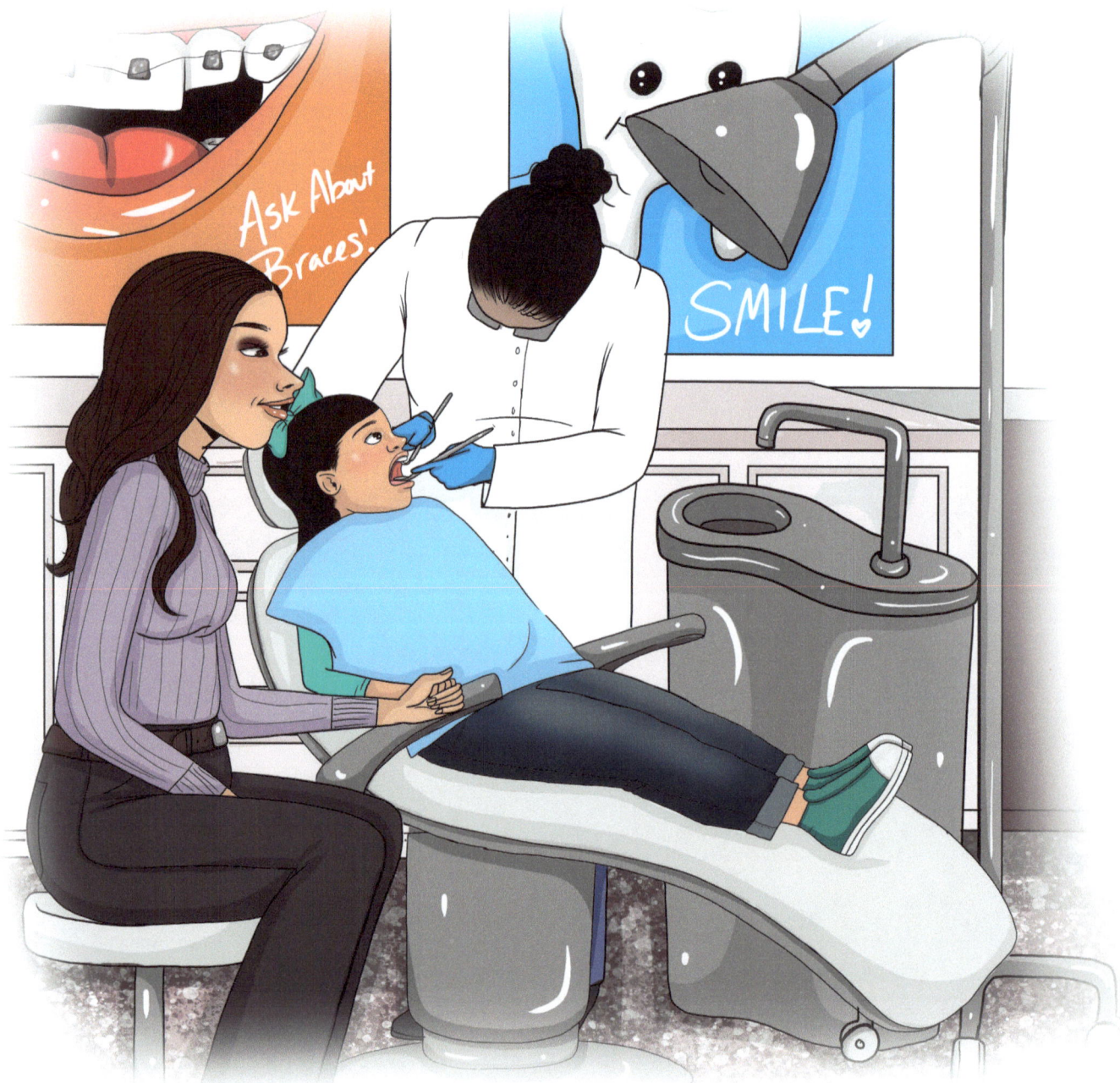

she soon relaxed her grip as she started to feel comfortable in the dentist's chair, learning about the benefits of regular dental checkups.

For her first camping trip, Dona decided to wear a **shimmering white bow** from her collection. Though she had originally feared sleeping in a tent in the dark, the camping trip was amazingly enjoyable as she gazed at the stars with her brothers and parents, warmed by a gentle campfire and soothed by song .

Dona had felt intimidated about getting behind the wheel with her father in the family car to learn to drive. But her fears subsided after she donned her collection's spotted **BLACK AND WHITE BOW**. Suddenly, she was up for the adventure and did remarkably well.

Dona was naturally nervous when a friend asked her out. After putting on a LIGHT BLUE BOW from her collection, she could relax for the date and had a wonderful time.

Dona wanted to be "psyched" for her first big English class test in high school. She discovered that wearing a **JET-BLACK BOW** increased her confidence, giving her the sense that the answer to every question was clear.

When trying out for the Golf team, Dona selected the rich **BROWN BOW** from her dresser drawer. It seemed to give her strength, as she knocked the ball down the fairway.

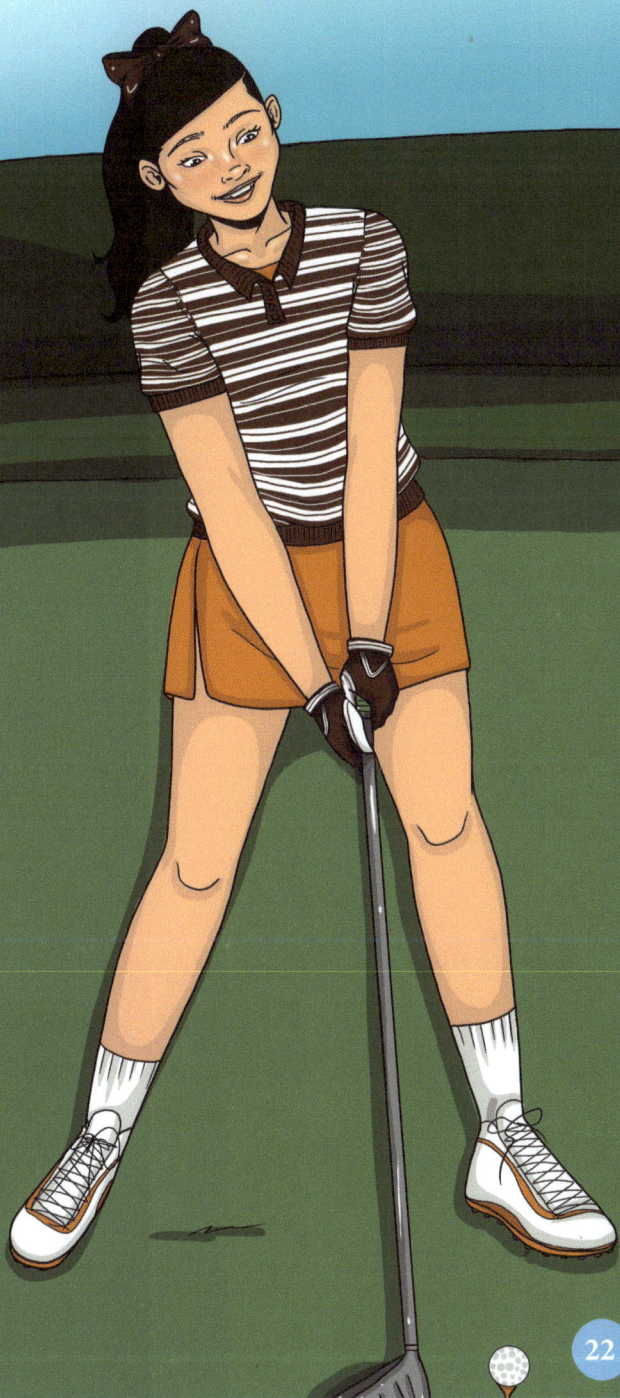

On the day of Dona's high school graduation, she wondered how she would perform as a leader of her class. Wearing the bright GOLD BOW from her collection,

she confidently made her way to the podium and delivered an inspiring speech, to enthusiastic applause.

Though Dona may still get a little nervous at times, she takes comfort in knowing that she can always draw upon her magical bow collection for support.

Dona's collection of bows comes in various colors, each symbolizing the courage to conquer fears and achieve her dreams. Join her on a journey through her youth and teen years, discovering that with a little courage, anything is possible!

Even if you don't have a magical bow collection like Dona, her story can inspire you to believe in yourself and your abilities. Whatever you choose to wear—or even just think—can be a source of streng th and confidence as you navigate your own challenges.

The Girl & Her Magic Bows

_ By Donatella DeLaRosa

MISNER AND MONROE PUBLISHING

Donatella is a high school student who is passionate about golf, dance, taekwondo, and connecting with people. As an enthusiastic and compassionate individual, Donatella loves helping others, making them laugh, and bringing people together. She is a leader in her community and school, known for her friendly nature and ability to inspire those around her. Donatella is also a wonderful sister and a devoted friend who cherishes her time with her two beloved dogs, Margarita and Tequila. Her vibrant personality and dedication to making a positive impact shine through in everything she does.

The Girl & Her Magic Bows

_ By Donatella DeLaRosa

MISNER AND MONROE PUBLISHING